Rhythm of Rest Study Manual

Kerrick Butler

Copyright 2025–Kerrick Butler

All rights reserved. This book is protected by the copyright laws of the United States of America. This book may not be copied or reprinted for commercial gain or profit. The use of short quotations or occasional page copying for personal or group study is permitted and encouraged. Permission will be granted upon request. Unless otherwise indicated, all scripture quotations are taken from the *King James Version* of the Bible. Used by permission. All rights reserved.

All emphasis within Scripture quotations is the author's own. Please note that Harrison House's publishing style capitalizes certain pronouns in Scripture that refer to the Father, Son, and Holy Spirit, and may differ from some publishers' styles. Take note that the name satan and related names are not capitalized. We choose not to acknowledge him, even to the point of violating grammatical rules.

Harrison House P.O. Box 310, Shippensburg, PA 17257-0310

This book and all other Harrison House's books are available at Christian bookstores and distributors worldwide.

Reach us on the Internet: www.harrisonhouse.com.

ISBN 13 TP: 978-1-6675-1352-2

ISBN 13 eBook: 978-1-6675-1353-9

Contents

1. The Sabbath — 1
2. Rest—God's Original Plan for Mankind — 9
3. Faith and Rest — 17
4. The Lord of the Sabbath — 25
5. Are You Working or Toiling? — 33
6. A.I.M. — 41
7. Opportunities of Rest — 49
8. What's Interfering with Your Rest? — 55
9. Rest Accompanies Victory — 63
10. Don't Live Off Beat — 69

About Kerrick Butler — 75
About the Publisher — 77

Chapter 1

The Sabbath

"Observe the Sabbath day by keeping it holy, as the Lord your God has commanded you. You have six days each week for your ordinary work, but the seventh day is a Sabbath day of rest dedicated to the Lord your God... Remember that you were once slaves in Egypt, but the Lord your God brought you out with his strong hand and powerful arm." (Deuteronomy 5:12–15, NLT)

You don't always notice you're close to burnout until the crash forces you into a pause. I remember the days when people would tell me, "I'll rest when I'm dead," as if rest were optional—something to earn after the hustle was done. But that mentality only hastens the very outcome we claim to accept. Statistics don't lie: millions of Americans suffer from chronic sleep disorders, burnout, and exhaustion, yet continue to operate as if running ourselves ragged is the norm. We're trading quality of life for an illusion of productivity, and it's breaking us down.

But God never meant for us to live that way. His design from the beginning was for us to live balanced lives. The Sabbath wasn't a last-minute rule tacked on to keep us in check—it was a vital part of His covenant with His people. He modeled rest Himself, not because He needed it, but to show us how to live. Rest was holy. It was a declaration that He had done enough, that the work was good, and now it was time to stop and enjoy it.

When I realized that my own body was showing signs of forced rest—fatigue, reduced clarity, slower recovery—it was a wake-up call. I was treating rest like a reward instead of a rhythm. And if the earth needed rest or it would force one, how much more would my body demand the same? We're made from the dust of the ground. Just as the land was forced into rest for seventy years due to Israel's disobedience, our bodies will eventually demand what we refused to give.

So I ask you: are you ignoring the signs? Are you in the cycle of pushing until you break, believing rest is weakness or laziness? Or will you accept God's invitation to live by His rhythm —the rhythm of rest?

Focus Point

"Therefore the children of Israel shall keep the Sabbath, to observe the Sabbath throughout their generations as a perpetual covenant. It is a sign between Me and the children of Israel forever; for in six days the Lord made the heavens and the earth, and on the seventh day He rested and was refreshed." (Exodus 31:16–17, NKJV)

This verse highlights that the Sabbath was not just a day of pause but a sacred sign of covenant —a visible token of divine agreement. The Sabbath represented more than rest; it was God's personal stamp of relationship and blessing. By keeping it, Israel acknowledged God as their deliverer and provider. When we honor rest today, we're doing the same—we're testifying that we trust the God who brought us out and will sustain us.

Main Theme

The Sabbath is not just about ceasing from work—it is about entering a divine rhythm. It was God's covenant sign to His people, and even though we're not bound to the law as the Israelites were, the principle still stands. Rest is a gift, a reflection of God's own example at creation, and a means of trusting Him with our time, our energy, and our outcomes. Whether it's one day a week or specific seasons in life, God calls us to live in the rhythm of rest. Failing to honor this rhythm leads to burnout, stress, and ultimately a forced rest. But embracing it opens the door to clarity, productivity, health, and alignment with His purpose.

"Rest is not weakness—it is obedience to God's covenant rhythm for your life."

Key Scriptures

- *"Therefore the children of Israel shall keep the Sabbath, to observe the Sabbath throughout their generations as a perpetual covenant... and on the seventh day He rested and was refreshed." (Exodus 31:16–17, NKJV)*
- *"So the message of the Lord spoken through Jeremiah was fulfilled. The land finally enjoyed its Sabbath rest, lying desolate until the seventy years were fulfilled, just as the prophet had said. (2 Chronicles 36:21, NLT)*
- *"The Sabbath was made to meet the needs of the people, and not people to meet the requirements of the Sabbath." (Mark 2:27, NLT)*

Key Points

- **The Sabbath Is a Covenant Sign** God gave the Sabbath as a physical and spiritual sign of His covenant with His people, reminding them that He is the one who sanctifies and sustains them.
- **Sabbath Is More Than a Day** It isn't limited to a single day each week. God also commanded Sabbath years, proving that rest should be woven into the fabric of life and society.
- **God Provides During Rest** When Israel obeyed God's command to let the land rest, He promised to supernaturally bless their sixth year with enough provision to cover three years.
- **Forced Rest Is Real** When Israel refused to keep the Sabbath, the land itself received its rest during the 70-year exile. If you do not rest, your body may eventually force you to.
- **Jesus Is Lord of the Sabbath** Under the new covenant, Jesus clarified that Sabbath is not about religious rules but about meeting the needs of people. Rest is a gift, not a burden.
- **We Are No Longer Under the Law** While we learn from the old covenant, we are not bound to observe the Sabbath as law. However, the principle of rest remains vital and biblical.
- **Rest Is an Act of Faith** Refusing to rest may be rooted in fear or unbelief. When we choose rest, we declare that we trust God to handle what we cannot.

JOURNALING QUESTIONS

Journaling allows us to engage with God's Word on a personal level. When you write your thoughts, convictions, and realizations, you not only reflect but also remember. In this chapter, we've explored how rest was not merely a good idea—it was God's design. Your journal becomes the space where you can analyze your own rhythms. Are you aligned with God's pace, or have you fallen into cycles of toil?

As you respond to the prompts below, be honest with yourself. This isn't about guilt or condemnation. It's about uncovering where you've adopted cultural norms over Kingdom rhythms. Through journaling, you can begin to identify unhealthy patterns and receive God's vision for rest in your life. Your transformation starts with truth—and the Holy Spirit speaks in the stillness.

RECOGNIZING THE SABBATH AS COVENANT

How does understanding the Sabbath as a covenant sign affect the way I view rest in my weekly routine?

_____
_____
_____
_____
_____

ACKNOWLEDGING FORCED REST

Have there been seasons in my life where my body or mind was forced into rest due to burnout or overwork?

_____
_____
_____
_____
_____
_____

Discerning Modern Pharisee Mindsets

In what ways have I made rest legalistic or ignored it completely, and how can I move into the balance Jesus taught?

_____
_____
_____
_____
_____
_____

Rest as Faith in Action

Do I struggle to rest because I feel everything depends on me? What does that reveal about my trust in God?

_____
_____
_____
_____
_____
_____

Redefining Productivity

How might God be redefining productivity for me through a deeper revelation of rest?

_____
_____
_____
_____
_____
_____

Actionable Steps

Honor Rest as Holy
Choose a consistent day or time block each week to cease from work and treat it as sacred. Use it to refresh your soul and reconnect with God.

Evaluate the Warning Signs
Make a list of current symptoms (physical, emotional, mental) that could indicate you are already in burnout. Seek God's wisdom on how to recover.

Rebuild Your Rhythm
Create a weekly rhythm that includes intentional pauses. Don't wait for a vacation—schedule mini-Sabbaths that allow time to refocus and breathe.

Personal Reflection

God didn't create you to live in a constant state of exhaustion. His blueprint always included rest. As you reflect on this chapter, take time to examine whether you've surrendered to that rhythm or resisted it. Is your body showing signs of fatigue? Is your mind restless even when your body is still? Maybe God is calling you into a new kind of obedience—not through doing, but through trusting.

We often wear busyness like a badge of honor, but that badge will betray you. It is not sustainable. It is not spiritual. It is not sacred. God is inviting you to learn from His rhythm and walk in His pace. That pace includes rest. That pace includes peace. That pace restores you, not depletes you. If Jesus took time to rest—even in the middle of His ministry—why would we think we are exempt?

Have I trusted God enough to truly rest? Am I willing to lay down control and embrace His rhythm? What needs to change this week so I can step into the rest He offers?

_____
_____
_____
_____
_____

Closing Prayer: *Lord, I thank You for showing me the gift of rest. Help me to stop striving and to trust You with the pace of my life. Teach me to walk in the rhythm of grace and not the pressure of performance. I surrender my exhaustion, my fear, and my control. Let me rest in Your covenant love and rediscover the joy of simply being with You. In Jesus' Name, amen.*

Chapter 2

Rest—God's Original Plan for Mankind

"Therefore the children of Israel shall keep the Sabbath, to observe the Sabbath throughout their generations as a perpetual covenant. It is a sign between Me and the children of Israel forever; for in six days the Lord made the heavens and the earth, and on the seventh day He rested and was refreshed." (Exodus 31:16-17, NKJV)

There was a time when I didn't fully understand how vital rest truly is—not just as a physical need but as a spiritual discipline. Like many people, I saw rest as a break or luxury, not a divine strategy. But when I began studying how God created the world and how He intended His people to live, I realized something important: rest wasn't man's idea—it was God's original plan. From the very beginning, He wove rest into the foundation of creation. And He didn't just suggest it; He sanctified it.

In the Garden of Eden, Adam and Eve's first full day wasn't a day of work—it was a day of rest. That wasn't coincidental. God was teaching us that rest is not the result of exhaustion, but the foundation of productivity. Before toil entered the world through sin, mankind worked and rested in rhythm with God. There was no anxiety, no performance pressure—just divine harmony. When we forget this, we fall into cycles of stress and burnout, which were never God's will for us.

What impacted me most was the realization that forced rest happens when we reject God's invitation to restful living. Just as the land went into forced rest when the Israelites refused to obey the Sabbath, our bodies will do the same if we don't pay attention. You can't violate God's design and expect divine results. Refusing to rest is a refusal to trust—and faith without rest isn't really faith at all.

So here's the question: have you accepted rest as part of God's will for your life? Or are you living as if rest is earned instead of embraced? Until you fully understand that rest is sacred, you will continue living in a cycle of overexertion and disappointment. But if you'll align with His rhythm, you'll experience His blessing.

Focus Point

"For in six days the Lord made the heavens and the earth, and on the seventh day He rested and was refreshed." (Exodus 31:17, NKJV)

This verse emphasizes that rest was not only part of the divine process—it was honored by God Himself. When the Creator of the universe took time to rest and be refreshed, it wasn't because He was tired. It was because rest is a demonstration of completion, satisfaction, and trust. If we are made in His image, we too are designed to operate from rest, not to crash into it.

Main Theme

Rest is not a reaction to weariness—it is the foundation of fruitfulness. God built rest into the very beginning of human experience because it is essential to living a whole and obedient life. Before sin brought toil into the world, Adam's first full day was one of rest. This pattern reveals that we are meant to work from a place of rest, not collapse into it after exhaustion. When we reject this rhythm, we step outside of God's design, opening ourselves up to burnout and ineffectiveness. True rest is an act of faith, a sign of trust, and a celebration of covenant.

"Rest is not an escape from work—it is the starting point of Kingdom purpose."

Key Scriptures

- *"Then the Lord God took the man and put him in the garden of Eden to tend and keep it." (Genesis 2:15, NKJV)*
- *"It is vain for you to rise up early, to sit up late, to eat the bread of sorrows; for so He gives His beloved sleep." (Psalms 127:2, NKJV)*
- *"The blessing of the Lord makes one rich, and He adds no sorrow with it." (Proverbs 10:22, NKJV)*

Key Points

- **Rest Came Before Toil** Adam and Eve's first full day on Earth was one of rest. This shows us that God's plan for humanity begins with rest, not labor.
- **Work Was Never Meant to Be Toil** God gave Adam a job, but toil entered only after the Fall. Work and rest were always meant to operate together in rhythm.
- **Rest Is a Sign of Covenant** When we rest, we demonstrate trust in God's provision and His blessing. Rest is a sacred declaration of our faith in His care.
- **Refusing to Rest Is Living by Toil** Those who live in constant labor and anxiety are living under the curse of toil, not the blessing of the covenant.
- **Rest Reflects the Blessing** The blessing of the Lord produces without painful striving. When we're aligned with God's rest, we prosper without burnout.
- **Everyone's Rest Looks Different** Rest isn't a one-size-fits-all activity. It requires discernment, reflection, and intentional planning that suits your design.
- **Rest Is Not Laziness** The Bible condemns laziness, but not rest. Rest is strategic, spiritual, and sanctified. Laziness is avoidance; rest is alignment.

Journaling Questions

This chapter gives us a powerful invitation to rethink our concept of rest. Journaling is a perfect tool to begin that shift. By writing down what rest means to us and evaluating our current rhythms, we can identify whether we're truly living in step with God's plan—or simply surviving on autopilot. Journaling slows us down long enough to examine the patterns we're living in and provides space for the Holy Spirit to speak clarity into those areas.

If you're unsure of how to rest, that's okay. Everyone's rhythm is different. That's why journaling matters so much here—it helps you get to know yourself as God designed you. As you respond to these prompts, expect God to give you insight not just about your schedule, but about your soul.

Understanding Original Intent

How does knowing that rest was part of God's original plan for mankind change my perspective on taking time off?

_____
_____
_____
_____
_____
_____
_____

Work vs. Toil

Am I working from a place of rest, or have I slipped into toil and performance-based living?

_____
_____
_____
_____
_____
_____
_____

Identifying Your Rest Rhythm

What kind of environment or activity brings true rest to my soul, not just my body?

_____
_____
_____
_____
_____
_____
_____

Building Regular Rest

How can I begin incorporating consistent rest into my weekly or monthly schedule?

_____
_____
_____
_____
_____
_____

Personalizing the Sabbath

What does a "perfect day of rest" look like for me, and how can I make that a reality?

_____
_____
_____
_____
_____
_____

Actionable Steps

Define Your Rest Rhythm
Take 15 minutes this week to write down what makes you feel rested physically, emotionally, and spiritually. Start to identify patterns.

Schedule Intentional Rest
Choose one day or time block this week to slow down. Set aside activities that drain you, and replace them with those that restore you.

Challenge the Toil Mentality
Every time you catch yourself thinking, "I don't have time to rest," challenge that thought with the truth: "God gives His beloved sleep."

Personal Reflection

If God chose to begin mankind's journey with rest, we should ask ourselves what we've been starting with. Many of us begin our week with anxiety, pressure, deadlines, and fear—yet God began it with a pause. It wasn't inactivity; it was intentionality. And it was blessed. What would change in your life if you chose to honor rest the way God does?

There will always be reasons to keep pushing. There will always be things left undone. But your soul doesn't thrive on finished tasks—it thrives on faith. And rest is one of the greatest signs of faith you can display. When you choose to rest, you're saying, "God, I trust that You're working even when I'm not."

What is my current relationship with rest? Am I aligned with God's rhythm, or resisting it out of fear or pride? What can I shift this week to reflect trust in His original design for my life?

Closing Prayer: *Father, thank You for showing me that rest is not a reward but a divine rhythm. Help me to embrace the rest You have built into creation and to honor it as a reflection of my trust in You. Reveal where I've slipped into toil, and give me grace to restructure my life around Your pace. I receive Your rest—not just for my body, but for my soul. In Jesus' Name, amen.*

Chapter 3

Faith and Rest

"Therefore, since a promise remains of entering His rest, let us fear lest any of you seem to have come short of it. For indeed the gospel was preached to us as well as to them; but the word which they heard did not profit them, not being mixed with faith in those who heard it."
(Hebrews 4:1–2, NKJV)

I still remember the conversations I had in college when people would come to me unable to sleep. They'd been tossing and turning, mentally exhausted but unable to rest. They were believers—faith-filled, Bible-quoting Christians—but something wasn't connecting. So they'd knock on my door at night and say, "Your brother said I should talk to you." I'd sit with them and show them two Scriptures: Psalms 127:2 and Proverbs 3:24. Then I'd pray a simple prayer with them. And guess what? Every single time, they came back saying, "That was the best sleep I've had in years."

That experience marked me. It wasn't just that God gives His beloved sleep—it was the realization that rest is accessed through faith. That's when I began to understand that a lack of rest in our lives is often a sign of a lack of faith. Not the kind of faith we shout about in church or post on Instagram, but the deep, abiding kind of faith that leads us to trust God enough to stop striving.

We often quote Scriptures like "the just shall live by faith," but many of us don't live that way. We plan, we push, we perform, and then we collapse. And then we call that rest. But Hebrews 4 makes it clear that rest is a promise—and it's accessed the same way we access salvation, healing, or provision: by faith. The Israelites missed their rest because of unbelief, not lack of opportunity. They had the promise, but they didn't mix it with faith.

So here's the challenge: are you believing for God's rest as intentionally as you believe for His provision or protection? If not, you might be missing one of the most essential blessings available to you in this life. Rest isn't just what happens when the work is done—it's what fuels the work God has called you to do.

Focus Point

"So we see that because of their unbelief they were not able to enter His rest."
(Hebrews 3:19, NLT)

This verse pulls no punches. It reveals the root issue behind burnout, worry, and disobedience—unbelief. The Israelites weren't excluded from the Promised Land because God changed His mind. They missed out because they didn't believe. In the same way, many of us live without rest, not because it isn't offered, but because we haven't mixed the promise with faith.

Main Theme

Faith and rest are deeply connected. The Bible teaches that we are to live by faith—but that same faith must manifest as peace and trust, not constant motion. True faith leads us to plan with purpose, live with margin, and resist the trap of toiling in our own strength. Rest is not passive; it is the spiritual result of believing that God is faithful to do what He said. Rest means we've shifted from self-reliance to God-dependence. Without rest, our faith is incomplete, and without faith, we'll never experience the fullness of rest that God has promised.

"Faith isn't proven in motion—it's revealed in your willingness to rest."

Key Scriptures

- *"So we see that because of their unbelief they were not able to enter His rest." (Hebrews 3:19, NLT)*
- *"When you lie down, you will not be afraid; yes, you will lie down and your sleep will be sweet." (Proverbs 3:24, NKJV)*
- *"For indeed the gospel was preached to us as well as to them; but the word which they*

heard did not profit them, not being mixed with faith in those who heard it."
(Hebrews 4:2, NKJV)

Key Points

- **Rest Is Accessed by Faith** Just like salvation, healing, or provision, rest must be received by faith. The promise exists, but we must believe it's for us and act accordingly.
- **Refusal to Rest Is Often Unbelief in Disguise** When we believe everything depends on us, we reveal that we haven't fully trusted God to sustain what He's called us to build.
- **Faith Requires Planning** Rest doesn't happen by accident. It must be planned and protected, just like any other spiritual discipline.
- **Long-Life Beliefs Require Long-Life Habits** You can't believe for a long, healthy life while ignoring rest, diet, or your body's warning signs. Faith and works must go together.
- **Toiling Is Not the Same as Working** God has called us to work, not to toil. Toil is painful striving without peace. Work is purposeful, Spirit-led, and balanced by rest.
- **Faith Is Both Word and Action** It's not enough to say you believe in rest—you must act on it. That means creating space for rest and resisting the urge to fill every gap.
- **Faith-Filled Rest Defeats the Enemy** The enemy will try to keep you exhausted so you're too tired to fight. But faith-filled rest is a powerful act of spiritual warfare.

Journaling Questions

This chapter makes one thing clear: rest is a faith issue. Many believers say they live by faith, but their lives don't reflect trust. Rest isn't just a response to tiredness—it's a revelation of belief. Journaling through this chapter gives you a chance to uncover the areas where your beliefs and habits don't align. It also allows space for the Holy Spirit to show you where faith must replace fear or control.

Through journaling, you gain clarity on where your schedule needs realignment and where your spiritual muscles need strengthening. Don't treat this lightly. This is more than self-help. This is soul care. It's where faith gets practical.

Faith in Action

Where in my life am I claiming to live by faith but refusing to rest?

_____
_____
_____
_____
_____
_____
_____

Planning for Rest

Have I made room in my schedule to reflect a life of faith, or is my calendar built around anxiety and performance?

_____
_____
_____
_____
_____
_____
_____

Breaking Toil Patterns

What habits or mindsets do I need to confront that keep me stuck in a cycle of overwork and burnout?

_____
_____
_____
_____

Making Rest a Priority

What changes can I make this week to honor God's invitation to rest by faith?

_____
_____
_____
_____
_____
_____

Evaluating My Sleep Life

Have I treated sleep as spiritual? If not, what Scriptures can I begin praying over my rest?

_____
_____
_____
_____
_____
_____

Actionable Steps

Confront Short-Life Habits
Take inventory of your lifestyle. What are you doing that contributes to exhaustion, stress, or poor health? Commit to replacing one short-life habit this week.

Build Rest into Your Faith Confessions
Add Scriptures about rest, peace, and sweet sleep to your daily declarations. Declare God's promises over your life and body with confidence.

Create a Faith-Based Rest Plan
Write down a specific, faith-filled plan for rest this week. It could be a consistent bedtime, a tech-free evening, or a mental health check-in. Treat it as seriously as any other assignment.

Personal Reflection

Sometimes the loudest evidence of our faith isn't in how much we do—but in what we're willing to lay down. God never asked you to carry it all. He asked you to believe Him. That includes trusting that He will sustain you while you rest. You don't need to earn rest. You already have it. The question is—will you receive it?

Faith is about more than movement. It's about alignment. When you live in rhythm with God's rest, you find clarity, renewal, and perspective. You'll get more done from a place of peace than you ever did from a place of pressure. Let this be the season you stop toiling and start trusting.

Have I confused rest with weakness? What does my current lifestyle reveal about where my trust really lies? Am I ready to honor God by entering His rest and planning my life from a place of faith?

_____
_____
_____
_____
_____
_____
_____
_____
_____
_____
_____
_____
_____
_____
_____
_____

Closing Prayer: *Father, I choose to trust You. I don't want to live a life of performance, anxiety, or exhaustion. I receive Your promise of rest by faith. Help me to break free from short-life habits and align my actions with my beliefs. Thank You for showing me that rest is not a luxury—it's a covenant right. I enter into Your rhythm of grace today, in Jesus' Name, amen.*

Chapter 4

The Lord of the Sabbath

"Come to Me, all you who labor and are heavy laden, and I will give you rest. Take My yoke upon you and learn from Me, for I am gentle and lowly in heart, and you will find rest for your souls. For My yoke is easy and My burden is light." (Matthew 11:28-30, NKJV)

I remember seasons when everything moved fast—deadlines, ministry demands, family responsibilities. And while productivity seemed like a badge of honor, I quickly realized I was missing something vital. Not just a nap or a weekend off, but real, sustaining rest. I was working hard for God, but not necessarily walking with Him in rhythm. And then I read the words of Jesus again: "Come to Me... and I will give you rest." That moment shifted everything.

What I had been missing wasn't time management or better sleep habit—it was intimacy. Jesus didn't call us to a system; He called us to Himself. When He said He was the Lord of the Sabbath, He wasn't giving us a new law. He was inviting us into a new relationship. The Sabbath is not just a day—it's a person. Jesus is the rest our souls long for.

That truth silenced the voice of legalism that said I wasn't doing enough. It also silenced the lie that rest is for the weak. Jesus modeled rhythms of rest even in the midst of ministry. He pulled away, He paused, He refreshed—not because He was lazy, but because He was led. That's the pattern we're called to follow.

So I ask you: are you walking with Jesus in the unforced rhythms of grace, or are you carrying burdens He never asked you to bear? If you want to experience true rest, you'll have to follow the Lord of the Sabbath into a lifestyle that looks different from the world's grind—but infinitely more fruitful.

Focus Point

"Then He said to them, 'The Sabbath was made for man, and not man for the Sabbath. Therefore the Son of Man is also Lord of the Sabbath.'" (Mark 2:27-28, NKJV)

This verse reminds us that Sabbath was never intended as a burden to bear—it was a gift to receive. Jesus reframed the mindset of the Pharisees, showing that Sabbath was created to meet the needs of humanity. And as Lord of the Sabbath, He offers us more than a rest day—He offers Himself as the source of rest.

Main Theme

Jesus is not only our Savior—He is our Sabbath. In Him we find true rest, not through rules or ritual, but through relationship. Resting in Jesus means living in the unforced rhythms of grace, where we move at His pace and trust His timing. It's not about legalistic observance but about learning to walk with the One who invites us to come, to learn, and to live freely and lightly. Our rest is found in the presence of the Lord of the Sabbath—not in a calendar but in communion with Christ.

"Rest is not found in a rulebook—it's found in the presence of Jesus."

Key Scriptures

- *"Come to Me, all you who labor and are heavy laden, and I will give you rest... for My yoke is easy and My burden is light." (Matthew 11:28-30, NKJV)*
- *"The Sabbath was made for man, and not man for the Sabbath. Therefore the Son of Man is also Lord of the Sabbath." (Mark 2:27-28, NKJV)*
- *"Be still, and know that I am God." (Psalm 46:10, NKJV)*

Key Points

- **Jesus Is Our Sabbath Rest** He is the fulfillment of rest, not just the enforcer of a day. Real rest comes from Him, not just from unplugging or pausing.
- **The Sabbath Was Made for You** God didn't design rest to burden you, but to

bless you. Sabbath is a divine provision to protect your soul and restore your strength.

- **Pace Is Personal** The Holy Spirit will guide your unique rhythm—sometimes telling you to move quickly, sometimes slowly, and sometimes to stop completely.
- **Rest Is a Form of Obedience** When you obey the Spirit's leading to pause, you position yourself for clarity, renewal, and divine acceleration.
- **Legalism Kills Rest** Trying to "earn" rest through performance misses the heart of God. Rest is not a reward—it's part of your inheritance in Christ.
- **The Rhythm of Grace Is Individual** What refreshes someone else might exhaust you. Find your own rhythm with Jesus. Learn what stirs your soul and pursue that intentionally.
- **Stillness Is Powerful** God speaks in stillness. When you rest, you position yourself to hear Him clearly and walk in His wisdom.

Journaling Questions

One of the most important ways to receive the truth in this chapter is by slowing down enough to reflect with the Holy Spirit. Journaling gives you the opportunity to listen, not just write. Rest isn't about stopping physical activity alone—it's about being still enough to hear the Lord of the Sabbath speak into your life.

This chapter invites you to examine whether your current lifestyle reflects intimacy or independence. Are you really walking with Jesus, or are you running ahead of Him? Use this journaling space to recalibrate, reconnect, and restructure your pace. As you do, you'll discover a grace-filled rhythm that leads to fruitfulness, not fatigue.

Following the Lord of the Sabbath

Am I letting Jesus lead my pace, or am I driven by pressure, comparison, or performance?

_____
_____
_____
_____
_____
_____
_____

Redefining Rest

Have I viewed rest as a weakness or inconvenience? How can I begin to see it as a gift from God?

_____
_____
_____
_____
_____
_____
_____

Hearing in the Stillness

When was the last time I was still enough to truly hear God? What might He be trying to say to me now?

_____
_____
_____
_____
_____
_____
_____

Personal Rhythms

What are the patterns or times of day when I feel most aligned with God's peace? How can I build my schedule around those rhythms?

_____
_____
_____
_____
_____

Spiritual Obedience in Slowing Down

Is there an area of my life where God is asking me to pause or slow down, but I've been resisting?

_____
_____
_____
_____
_____

Actionable Steps

Pause for Presence
This week, take 10–15 minutes each day to do nothing but sit quietly in God's presence. No agenda. No requests. Just listen.

Sabbath Scheduling
Look at your week and mark out a block of time you will protect as rest. Let it be a sacred appointment with God, not optional.

Reject Legalism, Embrace Relationship
If guilt or religion has distorted your view of rest, write down what you're releasing (e.g., "Rest is not laziness") and what you're embracing (e.g., "Rest is part of my obedience and trust in Jesus").

Personal Reflection

Jesus didn't just tell us about rest—He lived it. He walked away from crowds, napped during storms, and even pulled His disciples aside for solitude. If the Son of God, in three short years of ministry, still made room to rest, how much more should we? Maybe the most spiritual thing you can do right now is breathe, slow down, and trust.

There's a reason the enemy wants you exhausted. When you're weary, you can't discern. When you're frantic, you don't hear clearly. But in the presence of the Lord of the Sabbath, you find clarity, peace, and refreshing for your soul. You weren't meant to run on empty. You were meant to walk with Jesus—freely and lightly.

What does it mean for me to truly walk with Jesus in every area of life? How might my life look different if I trusted Him to set the pace? What is He asking me to lay down today so I can rest in Him?

Closing Prayer: *Lord Jesus, thank You for being my Sabbath—my place of peace, my source of rest, and my rhythm of grace. I choose to walk with You instead of striving alone. Show me where I've been running ahead or carrying what You never asked me to bear. I receive Your invitation to live freely and lightly, trusting that You know the pace that's best for me. In Your name, amen.*

Chapter 5

Are You Working or Toiling?

"It is vain for you to rise up early, to sit up late, to eat the bread of sorrows; for so He gives His beloved sleep." (Psalm 127:2, NKJV)

When I first began examining the difference between work and toil, it hit me like a wave: I had been toiling in areas where I thought I was simply being diligent. There were seasons where I rose early, stayed up late, pushed through fatigue, and called it "faithfulness." But the results weren't peace—they were exhaustion, frustration, and sometimes resentment. I began to realize that what I had accepted as necessary grind was actually unhealthy striving. And it wasn't producing Kingdom fruit.

As I studied Scripture, I saw a different model—God's original design was work, yes, but work without painful toil. Adam was given an assignment before the Fall, before the curse. He was to tend the garden, walk with God, and operate in dominion. But once sin entered the picture, the ground itself resisted him. That's when toil began. Toil isn't about effort—it's about effort apart from grace. It's sweat without satisfaction, striving without peace.

That realization changed how I approached everything. I started asking myself regularly: Am I working, or am I toiling? Am I operating in grace, or in grind? And when I listened closely, I could sense the Holy Spirit showing me where I had crossed the line. If God gives His beloved sleep, and if His blessing adds no sorrow with it, then living a life full of anxiety and strain couldn't be His best for me.

So, I ask you the same question today: Are you working, or are you toiling? The answer might change not only how you live, but how long and how well you live.

Focus Point

"The blessing of the Lord makes one rich, and He adds no sorrow with it." (Proverbs 10:22, NKJV)

This verse is a divine litmus test. If what we call "blessing" is bringing sorrow, stress, and burnout, then it's not fully aligned with God's way. His blessing produces increase, but not at the expense of your peace. If your gain costs you your health or your home life, it may not be a blessing—it may be toil in disguise.

Main Theme

God has called us to work, but He never intended for us to toil. Work, when done in alignment with God's purpose and empowered by His grace, produces fruit without unnecessary strain. Toil, on the other hand, is rooted in fear, pride, and unbelief—it's an exhausting attempt to accomplish what only God can truly provide. Understanding the difference between the two is essential if we are going to live in God's rhythm of rest and avoid cycles of burnout, anxiety, and forced rest. Rest is not the enemy of purpose; it is the protection of it.

"Toil is striving without grace—rest is working with God, not just for Him."

Key Scriptures

- *"The blessing of the Lord makes one rich, and He adds no sorrow with it." (Proverbs 10:22, NKJV)*
- *"It is vain for you to rise up early, to sit up late, to eat the bread of sorrows; for so He gives His beloved sleep." (Psalm 127:2, NKJV)*
- *"Then the Lord God took the man and put him in the garden of Eden to tend and keep it." (Genesis 2:15, NKJV)*

Key Points

- **Work Is a Gift** God gave mankind a purposeful assignment in the Garden. Work is not a curse—it is sacred and part of our divine design.

- **Toil Entered After the Fall** The pain, frustration, and fruitless labor we associate with work came after sin. Toil is not God's intention—it's a result of separation from Him.
- **Toiling Is Counterproductive** You can rise early, stay up late, and still produce nothing of lasting value if you're operating outside God's grace.
- **Rest Is a Measure of Trust** Refusing to rest reflects a belief that everything depends on you. True faith allows you to stop, knowing God is still working.
- **Toil Ignores the Holy Spirit** When we fail to seek God's direction or ignore His prompting to pause, we begin to operate in our own strength—and eventually wear out.
- **Productivity Without Peace Is Not Success** Just because you're producing doesn't mean it's from God.
- **Rest Requires Intention** Like any spiritual discipline, rest must be pursued with purpose. You must plan for it, protect it, and practice it regularly.

Journaling Questions

This chapter calls us to audit our energy, motives, and patterns. Journaling helps us get honest about what's driving us. Are we operating in faith or fear? In purpose or pressure? It's easy to call something "God-ordained" because it's good, but if it's draining your soul, God might be asking you to surrender it.

Use this journaling time to expose the toil in your life and invite the Holy Spirit to realign you with Kingdom rhythms. As you listen, don't just evaluate what you're doing—pay attention to how you're doing it.

Identifying Toil

What areas of my life feel more like toil than work? What are the signs that I've crossed that line?

_____
_____
_____
_____
_____
_____

Holy Spirit's Guidance

Have I asked God how He wants me to approach my work and schedule? Am I giving Him room to redirect my efforts?

_____
_____
_____
_____
_____
_____

Evaluating the Fruit

Am I producing results with peace, or have I been sacrificing my well-being in the name of "getting things done"?

_____
_____
_____
_____
_____
_____

Confronting Control

Is my refusal to rest rooted in a belief that everything depends on me?

_____
_____
_____
_____
_____
_____

Personal Revelation

What part of this chapter convicted me the most, and how will I respond to it?

_____
_____
_____
_____
_____
_____
_____

Actionable Steps

Audit Your Activity

Look at your calendar and responsibilities. Highlight anything that consistently produces anxiety, exhaustion, or dread. Ask the Lord if this is toiling or grace-based work.

Replace Toil with Trust

Each morning, take 5 minutes to commit your tasks to God in prayer. Ask Him to guide your efforts and remove anything that's rooted in fear or self-reliance.

Schedule Rhythmic Rest

Don't wait until you crash. Begin implementing weekly "rest checkpoints"—intentional moments to pause, reflect, and be refreshed.

Personal Reflection

Toil is sneaky. It can wear a mask of diligence, faithfulness, or even ministry. But beneath the surface, it's always the same: striving without grace. God never called you to be a machine. He called you to be fruitful—and fruitfulness flourishes in rest, not in frenzy.

Your body was designed to rest. Your spirit thrives when it trusts. And your purpose is best fulfilled when you're working with God, not apart from Him. Don't wait for a health scare, emotional collapse, or spiritual burnout to force you into reevaluation. Let the Holy Spirit recalibrate your rhythm now.

What is motivating my effort—trust or fear? Am I working from overflow or depletion? How can I realign my work with the grace and pace of God today?

Closing Prayer: *Father, thank You for showing me the difference between working and toiling. I don't want to live from a place of pressure, anxiety, or fear. Teach me how to operate in Your grace, to trust in Your provision, and to rest in Your promises. Help me surrender every area where I've been striving in my own strength. May I work with You, not just for You. In Jesus' Name, amen.*

Chapter 6

A.I.M.

"Set your mind on things above, not on things on the earth. For you died, and your life is hidden with Christ in God." (Colossians 3:2–3, NKJV)

There's a pattern I've seen not just in others—but in myself. When life feels out of control, we often respond by doing more, moving faster, or filling every gap in our schedule. But instead of peace, we end up exhausted. In one of those hectic seasons, God began to show me that the issue wasn't just my pace—it was my aim. I had been aiming at good things, even godly things, but without clarity, priority, or focus. That's when He gave me the acronym A.I.M.—Acknowledge, Inquire, and Meditate.

This isn't a motivational slogan—it's a spiritual tool. A.I.M. became the framework through which I could realign with God's heart and rhythm. *Acknowledge* meant slowing down long enough to recognize God's presence and admit my need for His guidance. *Inquire* meant asking the Holy Spirit honest questions and listening for His answers. *Meditate* meant sitting with His Word—not rushing through it—until His truth settled deep in my spirit. When I began to live by A.I.M., I saw fruit, not fatigue.

So many of us are busy without aim. We're making moves but not making progress. When we don't live with intention, we drift into overwhelm. But God calls us to live on purpose, with focus and direction. That's what A.I.M. gives you—a biblical, Spirit-led way to steward your mind, emotions, and priorities.

So let me ask you: Are you acknowledging God in your day-to-day? Are you inquiring of Him before reacting? Are you meditating on His Word or just rushing past it? If not, don't feel condemned—just come back to the posture of A.I.M. With the Holy Spirit's help, you can recalibrate and step into peace and purpose.

Focus Point

"Therefore I run thus: not with uncertainty. Thus I fight: not as one who beats the air." (1 Corinthians 9:26, NKJV)

Paul understood the importance of intentionality. He didn't live aimlessly or serve reactively. He ran with vision, fought with clarity, and lived with purpose. That's what A.I.M. empowers you to do—not just to move, but to move in alignment with God. Acknowledge reminds us to first recognize God's presence and sovereignty in every situation. Inquire encourages us to seek His wisdom before we act, rather than rushing ahead in our own strength. Meditate calls us to reflect on His Word and His voice, allowing truth to shape our thoughts and guide our decisions. This kind of spiritual aim doesn't come from ambition—it comes from awareness. It's not about doing more; it's about doing what matters most in the presence of the One who knows the end from the beginning.

Main Theme

To live in the rhythm of rest, you must aim your life with intention. A.I.M.—Acknowledge, Inquire, Meditate—is a spiritual framework to help you walk out divine strategy without striving. Acknowledge invites you to recognize God's presence and authority in every area of your life. Inquire draws you into deeper conversation with Him, seeking His wisdom before making decisions. Meditate anchors your heart in His Word, allowing His truth to shape your pace and priorities. Rest isn't passive—it's purposeful. When you acknowledge God in all your ways, inquire of Him continually, and meditate on His promises, rest becomes a rhythm, not a reward.

"You won't hit a target you don't aim at—purposeful rest requires intentional pursuit."

Key Scriptures

- *"Set your mind on things above, not on things on the earth." (Colossians 3:2, NKJV)*
- *"But be doers of the word, and not hearers only, deceiving yourselves." (James 1:22, NKJV)*

- *"Let us examine our ways and test them, and let us return to the Lord." (Lamentations 3:40, NKJV)*

Key Points

- **Acknowledge: Recognize God's Presence and Priority** Before you act, acknowledge God in every area of your life. This means humbly submitting your plans, emotions, and desires to His authority. Acknowledging Him sets the foundation for clarity and invites His presence into your process.
- **Inquire: Seek His Voice Before You Move** Inquire of the Lord with sincerity and patience. Don't assume—ask. When you seek His counsel through prayer and stillness, you position yourself to receive divine strategy rather than relying on assumptions or urgency.
- **Meditate: Let Truth Take Root** Meditation is more than reading—it's lingering with God's Word until it shapes your thoughts, actions, and responses. It creates space for peace, insight, and lasting transformation. Through meditation, rest becomes sustainable because your soul is anchored in truth.
- **Aimlessness Leads to Exhaustion** When you don't live on purpose, you default to reacting instead of responding. Clarity protects your peace. But clarity begins when you *acknowledge* where you are, what God is saying, and what needs to shift.
- **Rhythmic Rest Requires Strategy** Rest isn't random. It must be scheduled and secured. A.I.M.—Acknowledge, Inquire, Meditate—is a spiritual rhythm that helps you live intentionally. Acknowledge what's real. Inquire of the Lord. Meditate on His truth. Through this process, rest becomes part of your lifestyle, not just your escape.
- **Discipline Fuels Peace** Peace doesn't come from inactivity—it comes from alignment. When you *inquire* of God before moving, you walk in wisdom rather than impulse. That inquiry leads to discipline, and discipline brings sustainable peace.
- **Focus Guards Against Burnout** When your mind is anchored in truth, distractions lose their grip. *Meditation* focuses your heart and quiets the noise. It helps you stop overcommitting and start living with godly focus and intentionality.

Journaling Questions

This chapter shifts the conversation from principle to practice. A.I.M. is where the truth of God's Word intersects with the rhythm of your life. *Acknowledge, Inquire, Meditate* isn't just a mental exercise—it's a spiritual strategy. Journaling becomes essential here—not just for insight, but for intentional structure. You need space to think, pray, plan, and reset.

Let your journal be your strategic tool. Start by *acknowledging* where you are—emotionally, spiritually, and practically. Then *inquire* of the Holy Spirit. Ask Him to reveal what matters most in this season and how to move forward. As He speaks, *meditate* on what He shows you. Let it settle deep into your heart.

Write down what you hear. Let your journal hold the questions, the promptings, the confirmations, and the next steps. Revisit your entries often—not to micromanage, but to partner with God in living rested, fruitful, and focused.

Acknowledging Alignment

Am I honestly acknowledging where I am in this season? Have I become busy but unfruitful, or am I walking in step with God's plan?

_____
_____
_____
_____
_____

Inquiring for Clarity

What questions do I need to bring before the Lord right now? What has He shown me that I've been hesitant to ask more about or obey?

_____
_____
_____
_____
_____

Meditating for Renewal

Am I making time to meditate on what God has already spoken? How can I let His truth reshape my perspective and bring peace?

_____
_____
_____
_____
_____
_____

Purposeful Scheduling

How can I use *Acknowledge, Inquire, Meditate* to design a rhythm that includes both movement and margin—progress and rest?

_____
_____
_____
_____
_____
_____

Eliminating Aimlessness

What activities or habits am I engaging in that lack purpose? What do I need to release in order to live more intentionally?

_____
_____
_____
_____
_____
_____

Actionable Steps

Acknowledge What's True
Spend time in prayer this week asking God to help you honestly *acknowledge* where you are—spiritually, emotionally, and practically. Write down any patterns, burdens, or areas of drift He reveals. Let this become your starting point for alignment.

Inquire of the Lord
Bring your questions before God. Ask Him to clarify His priorities for this season and show you the next right step. Then choose one insight or instruction and take action on it—no matter how small. Obedience begins with inquiry.

Meditate with Intention
Set aside a weekly or monthly time to *meditate* on what God has spoken. Reflect on what's working, what's not, and where your heart needs recalibration. Let His Word and presence renew your focus and restore your balance.

Personal Reflection

Rest doesn't come by chance—it comes by choice. It's cultivated through *honest acknowledgment*, guided by *spiritual inquiry*, and sustained through *intentional meditation*. You can't expect peace if you don't pursue it. But the beauty of God's grace is that He equips us with the rhythms we need to live the life He designed.

A.I.M. is more than a method—it's a mindset. *Acknowledge* where you truly are. *Inquire* of the Lord for what comes next. *Meditate* on His Word until it transforms how you think and live. This rhythm teaches you to live on purpose, not just in motion. It breaks the cycle of reacting to life's chaos and empowers you to live from a place of peace.

So take your life off autopilot. Re-engage your heart. Acknowledge your present reality, inquire of God's direction, and meditate until your spirit aligns with His. Then move forward with clarity.

Am I willing to slow down long enough to acknowledge what's really happening inside me? Will I inquire of the Lord before I act—or keep relying on my own strength? How can I create space to meditate on His truth and let it anchor my pace and protect my peace?

Closing Prayer: *Father, I don't want to live aimlessly. I want to walk in step with Your Spirit, aligned with Your purpose, and anchored in Your peace. Teach me to aim my life with intention. Help me implement what You've spoken, and monitor my ways with grace and wisdom. May my life reflect focus, not frenzy, and may rest become a rhythm that fuels every step. In Jesus' Name, amen.*

Chapter 7

Opportunities of Rest

"Come to Me, all you who labor and are heavy laden, and I will give you rest. Take My yoke upon you and learn from Me, for I am gentle and lowly in heart, and you will find rest for your souls."
(Matthew 11:28-29, NKJV)

"There have been many moments when I have pushed myself to the edge. The calendar was full, the emails were endless, and the demands just kept piling up. But in the midst of one of those times of chaos, I realized that I had a choice. God was offering me rest. It wasn't a command to stop everything—it was an invitation to step into rest. That moment marked a shift in my understanding. Rest wasn't just something I crashed into after burnout. It was a continual opportunity offered by a loving God."

Rest isn't passive—it's intentional. We must choose it. And when we do, we discover that God has already created divine moments and windows of rest for us. These "opportunities of rest" aren't reserved for vacation days or rare sabbaticals. They're built into the rhythm of life when we listen to His leading and align with His pace. But if we don't recognize or honor those moments, we miss out on restoration.

Jesus offered rest to those who were weary—not just physical rest, but soul rest. And He still does. These opportunities aren't just about naps or time off work. They're about reconnecting with God, with peace, and with purpose. They're moments that recalibrate your spirit and remind you that you're not a machine—you're a beloved child of God.

What if we stopped treating rest as a reward and started treating it as a responsibility? What if we viewed each opportunity for rest as sacred—an appointment with God Himself to be refreshed and realigned?

Focus Point

"He makes me to lie down in green pastures; He leads me beside the still waters. He restores my soul." (Psalm 23:2-3, NKJV)

This verse captures God's active role in providing rest. He doesn't just suggest it—He *leads* us to it. He *makes* us lie down because He knows we won't do it on our own. Rest isn't an interruption in the journey—it's part of the journey, where He restores what the journey takes.

Main Theme

God provides continual opportunities for rest, but we must be willing to receive them. These moments are not random—they are intentional, sacred, and necessary for sustaining us in our purpose. Jesus modeled rest even in the midst of ministry, withdrawing to be with the Father and recharging His spirit. If He needed rest, how much more do we? True rest is not about inactivity—it is about intimacy with God and trust in His provision. Resting becomes a declaration that we believe God is working, even when we are not.

"Every opportunity to rest is an invitation to trust God more deeply."

Key Scriptures

- *"Come to Me, all you who labor and are heavy laden, and I will give you rest."* (Matthew 11:28, NKJV)
- *"Be still, and know that I am God."* (Psalm 46:10, NKJV)
- *"And He said to them, 'Come aside by yourselves to a deserted place and rest a while.'"* (Mark 6:31, NKJV)

Key Points

- **Rest Is an Invitation, Not a Punishment** God never forces us to rest out of condemnation—He offers it as a gift of grace to a weary soul.
- **Jesus Modeled Rhythmic Rest** Jesus intentionally withdrew from the crowds to rest and be with the Father. If He prioritized it, so must we.

- **Rest Renews Perspective** When we pause, we're able to hear more clearly, see more accurately, and think more soberly. Rest restores clarity.
- **Ignoring Rest Opens the Door to Burnout** When we resist God's opportunities for rest, we increase our vulnerability to stress, fatigue, and discouragement.
- **Rest Is a Form of Trust** Resting is an act of faith that God can handle what we've released to Him. It's declaring we trust His hands over our hustle.
- **Opportunities of Rest Require Discernment** Not all free time is restorative. True rest requires spiritual discernment to recognize God-ordained moments of replenishment.
- **Rest Is for the Journey, Not Just the Destination** Rest isn't just for recovery—it's part of endurance. It sustains you so you can finish strong.

Journaling Questions

Journaling helps you recognize the rhythm of God in your own life. Through this chapter, you're invited to identify where God may be offering you moments of rest—perhaps in simple, unexpected ways. The discipline of writing gives space to reflect on how you've responded to those invitations in the past and how you can embrace them moving forward.

Use this moment to get honest. Have you ignored or resisted rest? Have you believed the lie that constant movement equals significance? Let this be the point where you reconnect with God's pace and begin living out the truth that rest is sacred and available.

Recognizing Rest Opportunities

Have I noticed any recent moments where God was offering me rest, but I ignored or bypassed them?

_____
_____
_____
_____
_____
_____
_____

Rest as Trust

What is one area of my life where choosing rest would be a greater act of faith than continuing to push forward?

_____
_____
_____
_____
_____
_____

Jesus' Example

How can I practically follow Jesus' model of withdrawing to rest and reconnect with the Father?

_____
_____
_____
_____
_____
_____

Redefining Productivity

Do I define my value by how much I accomplish? What would it look like to redefine productivity through God's eyes?

_____
_____
_____
_____
_____
_____

Welcoming God's Rest

What is one way I can begin to receive God's invitation to rest more fully this week?

_____
_____
_____
_____
_____
_____

Actionable Steps

Create Space for Stillness
Carve out 15–30 minutes each day this week to disconnect from noise and simply be with God. Let Him recalibrate your heart.

Say "No" Without Guilt
Identify one commitment you need to pause or decline this week in order to honor your need for rest.

Plan Your Rest Before You Plan Your Work
This week, schedule your rest into your calendar first—not last. Treat it like a non-negotiable meeting with God.

Personal Reflection

Rest doesn't happen by default—it happens by design. The God who formed the universe also formed moments in your life to pause, breathe, and reconnect. When you step into those moments, you're not being lazy—you're being obedient.

You were not made to burn out. You were made to walk with God, at His pace, with His presence. And part of that journey includes stopping. Don't just push through life—pause through it. In those pauses, you'll hear Him more clearly and feel Him more closely.

Have I embraced the sacredness of rest? Am I trusting God enough to pause? What opportunities for rest is He offering me right now—and will I say yes?

Closing Prayer: *Father, thank You for creating opportunities of rest just for me. I repent for the times I've ignored or resisted those moments. Teach me to recognize the sacredness of rest. Help me to trust You more deeply—to believe that You are working, even when I'm not. Lead me beside still waters and restore my soul. In Jesus' Name, amen.*

Chapter 8

What's Interfering with Your Rest?

"Therefore, since a promise remains of entering His rest, let us fear lest any of you seem to have come short of it." (Hebrews 4:1, NKJV)

"I remember a night in particular where I had worked a long and full day. It was productive. I did everything I was supposed to do plus some more. I spent quality time with my wife and kids. After putting the kids to sleep, it was my time to enjoy and rest. However, I felt guilty about resting. I kept struggling with the thought of getting more work done. I realized that wasn't a healthy mindset. My mindset was interfering with my rest. What is interfering with yours?

Sometimes, the greatest barriers to rest aren't external—they're internal. We often blame our calendars or obligations, but the deeper issue is the clutter we carry in our souls: anxiety, unresolved offense, fear, performance mentality. These aren't just emotional weights; they are spiritual blockers. And if we don't identify and remove them, rest will always feel out of reach.

God has already offered us rest. The promise remains. But Hebrews 4:1 tells us it's possible to fall short of that promise—not because God failed, but because we didn't enter in. Rest is not automatic. It requires spiritual awareness and intentional surrender. The things that interfere with our rest are often subtle, disguised as responsibility or even spirituality, but they rob us of peace.

What is interfering with your rest? This is a necessary question for every believer. Not just to manage stress—but to pursue wholeness. If you feel stuck, overwhelmed, or unrested, don't just pray harder—pause, listen, and discern what's in the way. Because God's rest isn't far—it's just on the other side of surrender.

Focus Point

"Cast all your anxiety on Him because He cares for you." (1 Peter 5:7, NKJV)

This verse is an invitation to release what you were never meant to carry. Anxiety interferes with rest because it is rooted in control. But God offers to take your burdens—not just so you can survive, but so you can rest in His care.

Main Theme

Rest is available to every believer, but many never enter into it because they are entangled in spiritual and emotional interference. These interferences—such as fear, guilt, comparison, and striving—act as barriers that cloud our ability to trust God and receive His peace. Identifying and removing these obstacles requires honest introspection and a willingness to surrender. Only when these interferences are brought into the light can we truly embrace the rest God provides. True rest is not about external conditions; it's about internal clarity and divine trust.

"Rest isn't just found in what you stop doing—it's found in what you stop carrying."

Key Scriptures

- *"Therefore, since a promise remains of entering His rest, let us fear lest any of you seem to have come short of it." (Hebrews 4:1, NKJV)*
- *"You will keep him in perfect peace, whose mind is stayed on You, because he trusts in You." (Isaiah 26:3, NKJV)*
- *"Come to Me, all you who labor and are heavy laden, and I will give you rest." (Matthew 11:28, NKJV)*

Key Points

- **Rest Is a Promise, Not a Perk** God has already made rest available to His people—it's not earned through performance, but accessed through faith.
- **Interference Hides Behind Busyness** We often think we're just busy, but busyness can mask deeper issues like anxiety, approval-seeking, and spiritual avoidance.

- **Soul Clutter Blocks Spiritual Clarity** Unforgiveness, offense, and internal noise cloud your ability to hear God and settle into peace.
- **Fear Is a Thief of Rest** Fear keeps you in striving mode. When you fear lack, rejection, or failure, rest feels irresponsible—but it's exactly what God commands.
- **Performance-Based Christianity Is Exhausting** When your identity is rooted in doing rather than being, rest will always feel like failure instead of obedience.
- **Rest Requires Internal Surrender** It's not just about slowing your body; it's about quieting your soul. Rest begins when control ends.
- **The Holy Spirit Reveals What's Blocking You** You may not know what's interfering with your rest, but the Spirit does—and He lovingly exposes it to bring you freedom.

Journaling Questions

This chapter is one of confrontation and invitation. It invites you to examine what's truly keeping you from entering rest. Journaling will help you pinpoint areas of interference and allow the Holy Spirit to speak into them. Don't rush this process—let it be surgical.

Reflection is not about shame—it's about healing. When you write down the things that are cluttering your soul, you make space for God to address them. You might be surprised by what's been weighing you down. But freedom is always on the other side of truth. And truth comes through honesty.

Identifying Interference

What internal or external weights have been interfering with my ability to enter into God's rest?

_____
_____
_____
_____
_____
_____
_____

The Fear Factor

Is fear—of failure, lack, rejection, or the unknown—keeping me from trusting God enough to rest?

_____
_____
_____
_____
_____
_____

Performance vs. Presence

Do I feel more valuable when I'm busy and producing? How can I shift my identity from doing to being?

_____
_____
_____
_____
_____
_____

Cluttered Soul Inventory

Are there unresolved emotions, offenses, or responsibilities I need to release to the Lord?

_____
_____
_____
_____
_____
_____

Holy Spirit's Insight

What is the Holy Spirit showing me that I've been carrying unnecessarily—and how can I lay it down?

_____
_____
_____
_____
_____
_____

Actionable Steps

Conduct a Soul Detox
Set aside time to journal every emotional and spiritual burden you're carrying. Then, one by one, surrender each to God in prayer.

Speak Rest Over Your Life
Declare scriptures about rest, peace, and trust over your life daily this week. Let the Word cleanse the interference from your mind.

Create Boundaries Around Rest
Establish one boundary to protect your rest time—whether that's unplugging, saying no, or honoring Sabbath space.

Personal Reflection

You were not created to live in chaos. You were created to walk in divine rhythm, where rest isn't just occasional—it's continual. But to access that rhythm, you must confront the interference. Rest is still available. God's promise remains. The only question is—will you enter in?

The path to peace is paved with surrender. The things you're holding onto may be the very things keeping you from rest. But here's the good news: you don't have to carry them anymore. God is not asking you to fix it all—He's simply asking you to trust Him with it.

What is God asking me to lay down? What interference must I release to experience true rest? Am I ready to surrender, trust, and enter into His promise today?

Closing Prayer: *Father, I thank You that rest is my inheritance. Show me what's interfering with the peace You've made available to me. Reveal every fear, burden, and false belief I've been carrying. I surrender them now. Teach me to rest not just physically but spiritually. Restore my soul, renew my mind, and help me live from a place of holy rest. In Jesus' Name, amen.*

Chapter 9

Rest Accompanies Victory

"And the land had rest from war." (Joshua 11:23, NKJV)

I'll never forget when I first realized that rest wasn't something you only receive after the battle—it's something that accompanies victory. I began to see a pattern in Scripture: victory and rest are partners, not opponents. One of the clearest illustrations of this is Joshua. After years of war and conquest, Scripture says the land had rest. That rest wasn't the absence of struggle—it was the result of God's faithfulness."

In many people's minds, rest comes *after* the fight. We imagine we'll rest once we've conquered everything, checked every box, solved every problem. But that's not biblical rest. God's rest is different—it's peace in the presence of opposition, not just after it. In fact, real rest is part of the process that *brings* victory. It's not the reward for winning—it's the strategy that sustains us through the battle.

Joshua's generation teaches us that rest isn't passive—it's prophetic. It declares, "God has already given me the land, and I walk in that promise." When you rest in God's Word, you're not withdrawing—you're advancing from a position of strength. Rest is not retreat—it's confidence. And when you rest in Him, you're showing the enemy that your confidence is not in your strength, but in your covenant.

How would your life look if you truly believed rest was part of your victory—not something you earn after it? Would you still carry stress and anxiety, or would you walk with holy confidence, knowing the battle has already been won?

Focus Point

"Now thanks be to God who always leads us in triumph in Christ." (2 Corinthians 2:14, NKJV)

This verse reminds us that victory is not a possibility—it's a promise. God doesn't lead us into occasional wins; He leads us in continual triumph. Rest accompanies victory because God is the one leading, not us. And when He leads, victory—and the rest that follows—is guaranteed.

Main Theme

God's model for victory includes rest—not as a break from fighting, but as a supernatural force that operates alongside faith. When God gives victory, He also grants rest. Rest is not the absence of conflict but the presence of peace during and after it. We see this truth repeatedly throughout the Old Testament: when Israel walked in obedience and faith, God gave them rest on every side. Victory and rest go hand in hand because both are rooted in trusting God's provision rather than striving in our own strength. You don't have to wait for every problem to disappear before you walk in rest—you just have to walk with the One who already has the victory.

> **"You are not fighting *for* victory—you are fighting *from* it."**

Key Scriptures

- *"And the land had rest from war." (Joshua 11:23, NKJV)*
- *"And the LORD gave them rest all around, according to all that He had sworn to their fathers." (Joshua 21:44, NKJV)*
- *"Now thanks be to God who always leads us in triumph in Christ." (2 Corinthians 2:14, NKJV)*

Key Points

- **Victory and Rest Are Covenant Promises** God didn't just promise to deliver His people—He promised to give them rest. That's part of the inheritance.

- **Rest Declares Confidence in God** Choosing rest in a season of opposition says, "I trust God more than I trust my own effort."
- **Rest Is Not Inactivity—It's Stability** Rest doesn't mean doing nothing. It means doing what God has called you to do without striving or fear.
- **The Presence of God Brings Both Victory and Rest** Moses said, "If Your presence doesn't go with us, don't send us." God's presence brings assurance, direction, and rest.
- **Jesus Secured Our Victory and Our Rest** Through the cross, Jesus defeated every spiritual enemy and made a way for us to walk in supernatural peace.
- **Rest Is a Sign of Possessing the Promise** When Joshua led Israel to conquer the land, rest followed. That rest confirmed that the promise had been fulfilled.
- **You Fight Differently When You Know You've Already Won** When you understand that rest is part of the victory package, you stop striving and start declaring.

Journaling Questions

This chapter offers you a powerful paradigm shift. Journaling here will help you reframe how you view both your battles and your victories. Instead of seeing rest as a distant reward, begin to see it as a present reality that God is calling you into—right now.

Take time to ask yourself whether you've been striving to earn what Jesus already won. Reflect on where you've been working from fear instead of faith. God is not waiting for you to finish the battle to give you rest—He's offering it now, as you walk in trust and obedience. Writing these insights down will unlock clarity and strengthen your faith walk.

Covenant Understanding

Do I believe that rest is part of God's covenant with me, or have I treated it like a luxury I must earn?

_____
_____
_____
_____
_____

Warfare and Rest

How do I typically respond in seasons of spiritual warfare? Do I fight from peace or panic?

Victory Perspective

Have I seen rest as a sign of weakness or spiritual laziness rather than a sign of maturity and trust?

Following Joshua's Example

How can I practically walk like Joshua—conquering from a place of obedience and entering rest after each victory?

Living From the Cross

In what areas of my life am I still trying to win battles Jesus already conquered?

_____
_____
_____
_____
_____
_____

Actionable Steps

Speak Rest into Your Battles
This week, identify one area where you feel spiritually overwhelmed. Declare Scriptures of rest and victory over that situation daily.

Take a Faith-Based Sabbath
Set aside one day or portion of a day to rest with the intention of honoring the victory Jesus has already secured. Don't "earn" the rest—receive it.

Celebrate Your Wins with Worship and Stillness
When God brings you through something, don't rush into the next task. Pause. Celebrate. Worship. Then rest.

Personal Reflection

Rest is not the finish line—it's part of the race. As you walk with God, He weaves moments of stillness and peace into the journey to remind you that you're never fighting alone. The promised land isn't just about battles won—it's about rest received.

Stop striving to prove something God has already settled. Your job isn't to manufacture victory—it's to walk in what He's already secured. That walk includes seasons of warfare and seasons of stillness. Both are holy. Both are necessary.

Do I trust that rest is part of God's plan for me? Have I embraced the rhythm of rest that follows every victory? Am I ready to stop striving and live from the triumph Christ already won?

Closing Prayer: *Lord, thank You that rest is not a luxury—it's a promise. Thank You that victory and peace go hand in hand. Help me to stop striving and start trusting. Show me how to walk in the rest You've already provided. May every battle I face be met with confidence in Your Word and finished work. In Jesus' Name, amen.*

Chapter 10

Don't Live Off Beat

"Let us therefore be diligent to enter that rest, lest anyone fall according to the same example of disobedience." (Hebrews 4:11, NKJV)

So many of us live "off beat." We're rushing to meet deadlines God never gave us. We're stepping into seasons He hasn't prepared us for yet. We're worn out—not because life is too much, but because we've lost sync with His cadence. Like a song played too fast or too slow, something feels off in our spirit—and we can't figure out why. The issue isn't that God isn't speaking—it's that we're out of rhythm to hear and follow correctly.

God's rhythm for our lives includes both movement and rest. Just like music needs both notes and pauses to make a melody, our lives need both divine activity and holy rest. When we step outside of God's timing, even good things become burdens. His grace operates in rhythm, not in chaos. The enemy would love for you to stay busy—because busyness keeps you distracted. But when you walk in rhythm with God, you move with power, precision, and peace.

Are you living off beat? Are you sprinting through seasons God never designed for you? Or are you allowing Him to set the tempo of your life, even when that means pausing? If you've lost your rhythm, you can get it back—by listening to the Conductor and aligning with His timing once again.

Focus Point

"To everything there is a season, a time for every purpose under heaven." (Ecclesiastes 3:1, NKJV)

This verse is a reminder that God is a God of timing and order. He doesn't rush, nor does He delay. When we understand that every season has its appointed rhythm, we stop striving and start flowing. Being in rhythm with God means trusting His pace—even when it doesn't match our own.

Main Theme

Living off beat is a spiritual misalignment. It may not involve outright sin or rebellion, but it can still rob you of peace, power, and clarity. When you live outside of God's rhythm—when you ignore rest, overextend your yes, or take on burdens He never assigned—you invite exhaustion into your life. Scripture shows us that obedience is not just about *what* you do, but *when* and *how* you do it. God moves in rhythm, and He invites you to align with it. When you sync with His divine beat, you walk in sustained grace, discernment, and peace.

"God's grace flows best when you live in rhythm—not rush."

Key Scriptures

- *"Let us therefore be diligent to enter that rest, lest anyone fall according to the same example of disobedience." (Hebrews 4:11, NKJV)*
- *"To everything there is a season, a time for every purpose under heaven." (Ecclesiastes 3:1, NKJV)*
- *"In returning and rest you shall be saved; in quietness and confidence shall be your strength." (Isaiah 30:15, NKJV)*

Key Points

- **Off Beat Doesn't Mean Off Track—But It Can Lead There** You may still be following God, but moving at the wrong pace can open the door to weariness and confusion.

- **Rhythm Requires Relationship** The only way to stay in sync with God is to stay close enough to hear His leading. This isn't about rules—it's about relationship.
- **Your Yes Needs to Be Spirit-Led** Saying yes to everything—even good things—can cause you to live outside of God's assigned rhythm for your life.
- **Rest Is Part of the Rhythm** Without intentional pauses, you will eventually burn out. Rest isn't optional—it's vital to your spiritual harmony.
- **Peace Is a Rhythm Indicator** If you've lost your peace, you've likely lost your rhythm. God's rhythm is always accompanied by His peace.
- **Obedience Includes Timing** Delayed obedience or premature action can both lead to disorder. God's plan includes perfect timing, not just the right action.
- **Disobedience Can Be Subtle** Living off beat doesn't always look like rebellion—it often looks like self-directed busyness. But disobedience to God's rhythm is still disobedience.

Journaling Questions

This chapter is an opportunity to recalibrate. When you take time to journal, you slow down long enough to listen. Listening is where rhythm begins. God wants to reveal where you've gotten ahead—or fallen behind—and He wants to reset your pace.

Reflection invites you into divine realignment. It's not about condemnation, but correction. You might realize that certain things you thought were "urgent" weren't even yours to carry. As you write, let the Holy Spirit highlight areas of unnecessary pressure, hurry, and imbalance. Then, receive His rhythm—one of rest, clarity, and trust.

Recognizing the Misalignment

Have I been living off beat—rushing ahead or lagging behind God's timing in any area of my life?

_____
_____
_____
_____
_____
_____
_____

The Pressure to Perform

In what ways have I said "yes" to things that God didn't assign to me?

_____
_____
_____
_____
_____
_____

God's Rhythm vs. My Calendar

Is my current pace of life based on divine rhythm or cultural expectations and personal pressure?

_____
_____
_____
_____
_____
_____

The Role of Peace

Where in my life have I lost peace—and what might that reveal about my spiritual rhythm?

_____
_____
_____
_____
_____
_____

Recalibrating My Flow

What specific adjustments is God calling me to make so I can walk in sync with Him again?

_____
_____
_____
_____
_____
_____

Actionable Steps

Pause to Realign

Set aside 15 minutes this week with no agenda. Simply sit quietly before God and ask Him to reveal where you've moved out of sync with Him.

Audit Your Yes

Write down your current commitments. Ask God which ones are divinely assigned and which ones are crowding your rhythm. Release what He didn't give.

Plan Your Rest

Schedule regular rest into your week—not as an afterthought, but as a sacred appointment. Treat it with the same priority as any other assignment.

Personal Reflection

God's rhythm is holy. It's not dictated by urgency, pressure, or popularity—it's defined by peace, purpose, and presence. When we live off beat, we lose more than time—we lose sensitivity to His leading. But the moment we pause, listen, and obey, we can return to harmony.

It's not too late to get back in rhythm. The Holy Spirit is a faithful conductor, gently guiding you back to the divine pace. You were never meant to live in spiritual chaos or endless hustle. You were meant to walk to a beat that only heaven can give.

What rhythm have I been following—God's or mine? What would it take for me to fully surrender to His pace? Am I ready to stop performing and start flowing again?

Closing Prayer: *Father, thank You for being a God of divine order and rhythm. Forgive me for moving ahead of You—or behind You. I choose today to realign with Your pace. Teach me to live in sync with You, to follow Your Spirit instead of my schedule. Help me to find rest, strength, and peace in Your divine rhythm. In Jesus' Name, amen.*

About Kerrick Butler

Kerrick A.R. Butler II is an author, broadcaster, civic leader, and pastor. Kerrick serves as Senior Pastor of Faith Christian Center located in Mableton, Georgia. He is a graduate of Word of Faith Bible Training Center and Oral Roberts University. Kerrick believes wholeheartedly in sharing the message of Jesus through creative avenues to help people apply Bible truths to their everyday lives. Kerrick, his wife, Racquel, and their beautiful family reside in Metro Atlanta.

———

Harrison House is a Spirit-filled, Word of Faith Christian publisher dedicated to spreading the message of faith, hope, and love through our wide range of inspiring publications. Committed to the messages that highlight the power of the Word and Spirit, we provide books, devotionals, and study guides that empower believers to live victorious, faith-filled lives.

Our resources are designed to help readers grow spiritually, strengthen their faith, and experience the transformative power of God's Word. Harrison House is passionate about equipping Christians with the tools they need to fulfill their divine purpose and impact the world for Christ.

———

www.ingramcontent.com/pod-product-compliance
Lightning Source LLC
Chambersburg PA
CBHW080839230426
43665CB00021B/2891